Peg Masters Hathcock

ASAFETIDA:

that was my bag

by

Peg Masters Hobrock

DORRANCE & COMPANY
Philadelphia

To my late grandmother,
for the gift of her genes.

ASAFETIDA

Webster defines it as a bad-smelling gum rosin.

Believe me, it was sure bad smelling.

My mom never lost her faith in the asafetida bag.

Today, a little girl would wear a gold chain with a little gold heart.

I wore a horribly smelly asafetida bag on a string, guaranteed to ward off germs.

It only warded off the other kids whose mothers did not have the faith of mine. Maybe it warded off leprosy. I never had *that*. But name a so-called child's disease and I had it.

But my mom never wavered.

When my mother had faith, she had faith!

THIS CONCERNS THE LAND OF "NO"

No toilet paper
No bathrooms
No electricity
No sex. . . . You got to be kidding.

If you were born in a hospital instead
of the procreation bed, this is news.

If otherwise, this is memories.

WORDS WE DIDN'T KNOW

Tea Bag
Garbage Man (We buried it in the ground.)
Baby Sitter
Birth Control
Bodies (We knew we had them but we kept them
    hidden.)
Sex (It existed; we just didn't give it a name.)

WORDS YOU MIGHT NOT KNOW

Asafetida
Honey Dipper (has nothing to do with candy).
Medicine Man
Button Hook (No home could exist without one.)
Ferris Waist (If you were a fatty at age 12, you got
    encased in one of these—girls only.)
Teddy (This came with the 1920's as woman became
    liberated. A silk coverall undy.)
Rats (Hair puffs you hid in your hair.)

SEX SYMBOL

The first sex symbol I remember was Clara Bow (movie star) in "IT."

We actually didn't understand IT, but knew it had something to do with the opposite sex.

During the great Hollywood hullabaloo of promoting Clara, one of our great, beefy football players stood on the stage of the high school auditorium and, in the frenzy of the football rally, said in a screaming voice,

"I have IT, and I am going to keep IT."

For days, I searched my mind on how IT was going to win the football game.

We won, but I think it was because some of our boys didn't have birth certificates and took more than four years getting through high school.

That could have been IT.

SEX

Sex to us was like the moon in pre-space days.

We knew it existed, but actually what it was, was never mentioned in the home.

The word sex was not in our vocabulary until the 1920's.

If an unmarried girl produced a child, my mother acted like it was a virgin birth.

The kids learned the facts of life like putting together the pieces of a jigsaw puzzle; some really went all out piecing the puzzle.

These girls always had the boys hanging around, and the rest of us thought we must be ugly.

By the time we got to high school, all of us were beginning to get the picture, but the threat of producing children kept us moral.

Birth control wasn't even whispered.

We knew what bodies looked like because almost every home had an enormous doctor-book, and in it were bodies in sections like pages.

You saw the heart, the kidneys, etcetera, layer by layer, and it surely didn't look enticing.

When we finally were plunged into the whole bit on a wedding night, it was like WOW to some and WOE to others.

Immorality and divorces occurred in families, but, like our bodies, they were kept under heavy wraps.

I would say that in the early 1900's people were sneaky.

SEX DEVIATES

Homosexuals

If we had heard that word at home, we would have thought it was a foreign word or a new species of bird.

In my teens I got the message, but they were called "pansies."

Lesbians

That term didn't appear in my vocabulary for many years.

Prostitutes

This we vaguely knew as a "kept woman." One woman would appear in our neighborhood in a chauffeured limousine.

We were a Ford neighborhood.

Mother said she was a kept woman.

I thought, "How nice to be a kept woman," and wondered why the other mothers didn't aspire to be "kept."

I never asked why she was "kept."

THE CHANGE

That was what it was called.

To most girls—boom!—it was here.

What was it?

It was taboo time.

"Don't wash your hair!"

"Don't take a bath!"

You expected to be tortured. You were meant to suffer.

It was blamed on Eve.

For some reason you didn't understand, Mother became like a detective. Where were you? Who were you with?

Up to this time, you only had to be home in time to eat or go to bed. Being ignorant of the facts of life, we thought we had suddenly become important.

BABIES

Babies at *our* house came in the family doctor's bag. This event was always heralded by an exciting invitation to grandma's or an aunt's.

When we returned home, there IT was. IT was our surprise.

I could never understand why mom was allowed to lie in bed and a strange woman was doing her work—just because IT arrived.

My brother got so disgusted because the ITS were always girls, that one day he brought the mail-order catalogue to Mom and said, "Read this letter from a satisfied customer." The letter stated they had dealt with them for years and had seven boys. We had dealt with them for years and had only one boy. He felt she should send an order immediately for another boy.

He never won. His home life was made up of red-haired women—his mother and sisters.

CREDIT

Today, the only place you don't have a charge card is the local supermarket.

Then, the only place the average housekeeper had credit was the corner grocery store.

Your grocer was your security. When work was scarce (there were no unemployment checks, no welfare), your grocer kept you supplied until the paychecks started coming in again.

No family went hungry.

However, I am sorry to say that, even then, there were deadbeats, and few grocers ever got rich.

The grocer didn't charge you for credit. He gave you a bonus. The kids looked forward to payday. Mom paid her bill, and the grocer presented her with a red-and-white-striped bag filled with candy.

TRADING STAMPS

We had trading stamps in the far-away past, only we called them "premiums" or "coupons."

A smelly, yellow soap, that was a must for the family wash, had coupons that one cut from the wrapper.

My grandmother owned a tea company, and my dad drove the horses and wagon and sold the tea and coffee, and gave the premiums which are the antique pressed glass that is so valuable today. I wish I had some.

The Larkin Mail Order Company (which I do not think exists today) gave you extra credit on the amount you bought, and my favorite doll came to me that way.

We didn't have the Avon Lady—we had the Larkin Lady.

BRAND NAMES

The first thing a woman looks at (my husband says men do it too), when another woman lays her coat down, is the label.

This is a status symbol.

We had labels.

We carried the brand names of our mother's flour—unbleached muslin sacks.

Nothing came in paper bags. No good housekeeper wasted a bit of cloth.

Our slips and panties were not ornamented with lace, but the picture of a rooster could be seen on your posterior if a good wind was blowing.

THE ICEMAN

On a hot summer day we all awaited the coming of the iceman.

Every kitchen or pantry or back porch contained the ice box. This upright, square wooden container hungrily consumed a block of ice a day in order to keep the butter, eggs and milk—nothing was cold.

The icewagon was pulled by the dependable, knowledgeable horse who automatically stopped at every house. This was automation in that day. The iceman with his trusty ice pick chunked off a 25 or 50 pound hunk of ice, picked it up with a large black tong, placed it on his shoulder, carried it into the back of your home and dropped it into the icebox.

Meanwhile, out in the street, a happy pack of kids scrambled into the wagon, grabbing for the chips of ice that had fallen to the floor.

A happy iceman always left you large chips. He was our Good Humor man. We didn't know what an ice cube was. They came with the electric refrigerator.

I bet you are thinking, "Was that ice filled with germs? Was it dirty?"

Could have been. There was a saying at that time— "You have to eat at least a peck of dirt in your lifetime." So maybe we got ours early. We survived.

THE MEDICINE MAN

Summer brought to our small town the Medicine Man.

To me, he was Mr. Show Biz (in modern lingo). He showed up every summer in his covered wagon with the Indian—always the Indian. The Indian to us was like a man from Mars (except we didn't know about the Martians).

Our Medicine Man would only be in town a few hours, when he knew about the people with the tapeworms, and he would relieve them of their tapeworms and put them on display in large bottles of alcohol.

These long, horrid-looking white things that resembled spaghetti were one of the ailments he saved us from. He must have obliterated them from the face of the earth, as I never hear the word "tapeworm" today.

In the evening, the long-awaited event occurred. The Indian beat the tom-tom. All the neighborhood rushed to the vacant lot to see this (in our case, very handsome) beautifully dressed Medicine Man. In his super-salesman voice, he extolled the healing powers of his brown liquid that sold for fifty cents a bottle. (Fifty cents was a lot of money.) Not only would our tapeworms leave our bodies, but all other ailments would disappear—really, the stuff (I guess) *did* make you feel good. It had a good share of alcohol in it.

Everybody bought.

He also had a white soap. I don't know why, but he always beat soapsuds into water and drank it to show us how pure it was.

One summer, he didn't show. I was heartbroken, as he was my movie idol. I heard later that he died from drinking too many soapsuds.

THE BEER MAN

The Beer Man was as round as the kegs of beer he carried in his wagon (no cans or bottles). His horses were just as fat. He stopped at grandma's house down the block from us.

The whole family lived near grandma. She was the matriarch. She had brought her brood safely across the Atlantic from Wales (granddad had preceded her), and no one was leaving the shelter of her wings.

Saturday night was spent in grandma's enormous kitchen. No grandchild ever ran through grandma's house. We peeked into the parlor and admired the china vases on the mantlepiece, but the kitchen was the family room.

We had cheese and bread, and even the kids got a sip of beer. The grown-ups talked, the kids fell asleep, the younger ones got carried home, and the older ones walked in their sleep the few steps home.

The word "babysitter" hadn't been invented yet.

Then it happened.

Prohibition came in and granddad, always the law-abiding citizen, emptied his beer keg immediately, and that was the end of our beer man and the beer.

After that we only had tea, and it wasn't half the fun.

TERRITORIAL STAKEOUTS

We didn't have race problems. With a few exceptions, we were WASPs, but, of course, we didn't know it. But we did have the boy who felt the pioneering spirit, and dated the gal from the other part of town.

He knew it was dangerous. This was really the only danger he faced. So on Friday night, date night, he crossed the railroad tracks and walked belligerently to the other side of town so he would be noted by the boys as the alert sounded and the boys gathered.

Then, about ten o'clock (that was late), he emerged from the porch swing after kissing the gal goodnight and with his heart pounding (not from the kiss), knew that he had to face the dragon.

At the halfway mark, the boys were waiting, and the race began. If he was a fast runner, he made it to his side of the tracks; if not, he got a beating, not too bad. No one called the cops; this was just the natural way of life.

Actually, the thrill of dating the girl was not half as great as the thrill of being assailed by the enemy.

We had few delinquents, as this thrill of battle usually took care of any excess energy.

WOMEN'S LIB

There have always been liberated women.

My grandmother was one. She married at sixteen, produced sixteen children, some of whom died in childhood, as did many in that day, brought her remaining brood across the ocean in the late 1800's, and, in this new strange country, owned and managed a tea company, a restaurant, and several grocery stores.

Granddad worked in the mills, but Grandma ran businesses.

Another liberated gal in the early 1900's ran and owned the candy store that had a big, marble ice-cream-soda bar on one side and a beautiful glass case filled with luscious candy on the other. This was my favorite store.

Across from the candy store was a large grocery store managed by another modern woman (the word modern wasn't used in that day). This gal not only managed the store, but did all her own carpentry work.

These women never looked like workhorses. The were always attractively attired.

My grandmother had elegant clothes—heavy silks and satins, and always the beautiful white sheer apron, which I suppose was part of the Welsh attire.

FEARS

I had two—the fear of gypsies and the fear of God.

Mom gave me the first, and my Sunday School teacher the second.

Why the gypsies appeared every summer, I really don't know, but they did.

We didn't have a phone, radio or TV, but we had word of mouth. "THE GYPSIES ARE HERE!"

Mom called us to her bosom and said, "They are here, and they will kidnap you."

Why us? I wouldn't know, unless Mom, in her love, saw her red-headed, freckle-faced brats as golden angels.

But we believed her, and when we saw anyone we didn't know (and we knew everyone for blocks), we hid under the bed.

The fear of God, which was put into us every Sunday (Sunday School was just as much a must as grade school), lasted until Wednesday.

Everything that was enjoyable was sinful.

Years later, I'm sure a psychiatrist would have understood my many guilt feelings.

If I felt jealous of Mary because her hair ribbon was bigger than mine, I sinned.

"Jealousy is the ruination of the world," my teacher said, and I sure condemned myself every time I envied that girl with the golden curls.

DANGER

What would happen today if a luscious-looking piece of candy appeared on the market with a marble inside?

Headlines in the paper—TV screaming.

This was our favorite candy.

All boys and tomboy girls play marbles. This great big chocolate drop contained in its middle a marble. You took a chance on this. I guess we were gambling, but didn't know it.

As you bit cautiously into the middle, you were wondering, "Was it a kimmy (a nothing marble) or an agate (a beautiful glass marble)?"

I never knew a kid to choke on this tasty bit. We at the candy, too. Our generation was never over-suppli with sweets.

THE TELEPHONE

Can you imagine being frightened of the telephone?

The first telephones in our neighborhood were in the places of business. So, of course, grandma had one.

One day, my ever-present friend, who assisted me in my acts of devilment, and myself saw the opportunity to speak into this tall, black instrument. We knew of one other telephone. An oil man, whose daughter was our age, had it. We felt very brave as we lifted the receiver, and central said (they are called operators today), "Number, please."—we just gave the name, and the oil man answered.

We were petrified. Too afraid to talk, too afraid to hang up, and finally, after no answer from us, he cursed us in every term that a man working in the oil fields over the county had learned. We dropped the receiver and ran.

For days, we expected some dreadful event. We felt for sure we were known to be the ones who committed this terrible deed.

The telephone began to appear in private homes. Four party lines were the average.

This opened a whole new way of life to the housewife. Listening-in took away from the dusting.

Nothing took place in the lives of the four parties that wasn't known to each of them. But my mother had a weapon. When she talked to any of her family, she spoke in Welsh, and you could hear the receivers banging.

Next door to us lived two elderly ladies. A kind relative got them a phone. These two gals worked out a system. They were afraid to tackle this instrument alone, so one listened and one talked.

One day, they both got so frightened over the fact that they were in touch with someone on the other side of town, that they dropped the phone and ran out of the house and wouldn't return until this frightening instrument was removed.

BOOKS

The library in our home consisted of the Encyclopedia Brittanica, the complete set of Washington Irving's writings, and Alexandre Dumas's *The Count of Monte Cristo.*

This was our reading material.

However, kids were kids yesterday, and are today, and somehow I got hold of *Three Weeks* by Eleanor Glynn (about a clandestine love affair), and secretly read it in the stealth of the night.

This was considered the torrid reading of the day. I would imagine that today it wouldn't even qualify for sex education in first grade.

SIGNS OF OUR TIMES

We had pink, yellow, red. You name it—we had it! SIGNS—quarantine signs.

The minute Johnny came home from school with chicken pox, the health officer showed up. He must have had a radar antennae.

He tacked a sign on the front of the house for the world to see, and, in large black letters on a background of whatever color, designated the disease.

The neighbors were warned, and you, the healthy one, were treated like a leper.

So you might as well sleep with Johnny and get it over with.

Mom deliberately had the kids shake hands and breathe with Johnny so the whole household would get it over with.

After all, these were necessary evils, and it was better to get them when you were young.

Mumps, measles, chicken pox, whooping cough.

The only shots Mom heard of were gun shots.

Diphtheria and scarlet fever were dreaded. These were red signs.

Kids in large families lost so much time from school due to quarantine that if they graduated from high school by the age of twenty or even from grammar school, they were lucky.

We got promoted twice a year and that saved some of us.

SMELLS

I have often wondered what Friday was like in that hot schoolroom. Maybe it wasn't so hot, because central heating was not part of my early childhood.

Imagine a roomful of adults and kids who bathed only once a week. Bathing was weakening.

Saturday you got the weekly bath.

In the winter you wore long woolen underwear. Everyone—females and males. Females wore woolen slips and woolen dresses.

No one shaved under her arms (heaven forbid the thought). Deodorants didn't exist. Sweat did.

Now that I am reminiscing, I recall that twice a day in the coldest of weather, teacher opened the windows and we were told to stand up and breathe deep.

Now I understand.

I don't know how a germ had the guts to enter into us.

LONGIES

Can you imagine a girl today wearing long, lumpy underwear under heavy ribbed stockings, because it was the unwritten law of the home?

We rebelled then, but not openly.

As soon as we left the confines of our abode, we stopped right on the sidewalk, rolled down the hose, rolled up the underwear, and then pulled the hose up and hoped and prayed that the underwear wouldn't sneak back down on the outside of our leg—sometimes it did.

Our embarrassment was tremendous at this point.

We all wore elastic garters like rubber bands. It's a wonder we didn't all have premature varicose veins.

FLAPPER

In the 1920's, the four and six buckled boots became the rage. I was only allowed the four-buckle, but the excitement of waiting until you turned the corner and Mom couldn't see you, and you could open two, and, if you felt dangerous, three buckles, and could flap your way to school, made the day worthwhile. Hence, the word "flapper." The byword of the 1920's. Our world was opening up, for better or worse.

STREETCARS

Streetcars were a vital part of our life.

On Saturday nights, when the movies let out, our streetcars were not only packed, but men were hanging on the cow catchers (that's what they called the large metal protector on the front).

In the summer we had summer cars, open cars with benches width-wise. The motorman who ran the car knew the workers who rode, and if you weren't at the car stop in the morning, he waited for you.

The conductor collected your five-cent fare.

One of the men in our neighborhood who worked hard all week usually got inebriated on Saturday night. He somehow managed to get on the streetcar after leaving his favorite pub, and, as the car passed his home, the motorman would stop and the conductor conduct him right to his front door.

This was real service for five cents.

The first streetcar pass cost twenty-five cents for the whole week, and the favorite sport for the kids was to collect the pass from Dad or some kind soul in the neighborhood and then ride all Sunday afternoon or all day Sunday from one end of the line to the other.

The men who worked on the streetcars were your friends.

THE WEEK THAT WAS

For years, I thought the Constitution of the United States read:

Monday——Washday

Tuesday——Ironing day

Wednesday——Mending day

Thursday——Baking day (that was our bread)

Friday——Heavy Cleaning day (heavy is the word— no vacuum, no spray polish)

Saturday——Kids scrubbed the porches and the sidewalk, and then took off for the "shows."

Sunday——Sunday School day (you better believe it!)

WASH DAY

Monday meant washday.

Washday meant the horrible smell of chipped, yellow soap (soap powder was unknown) being boiled in a copper boiler.

The clothes were rubbed on a washboard and then boiled, then ladled out into a tub of rinse water, then put through a handringer; again, into a tub of rinse water containing liquid bluing (this bluing was also used to cure ringworm, which seemed to be quite prevalent); again, through a handringer and then hung on the line—winter and summer.

No wonder on washday Mom said, "Oh, my aching back."

However, in our neighborhood, there was a silent competition going on. It was a source of great pride to be the first to get those clothes on the line and have them the whitest.

A great new invention came into our home.

The hand-worked washer.

The kids got into the act. They turned the wheel that turned the agitator. Life was getting easier for the housewife.

One smart woman in our neighborhood put her wash into the washer on Sunday, and every dinner guest took his turn at the wheel. Of course, she couldn't hang her clothes until Monday, as she would have been disgraced to have her lines filled with clothes on a Sunday.

POLLUTION

Can you imagine a rug that spent a whole year on the floor without the suction of a vacuum cleaner? What good would a vacuum cleaner be without electricity?

The only cleaner this rug felt was the soft brush of the hand-Bissell.

In the spring, the rug came off the floor and onto the clothesline. Mom, Dad, and all the kids covered their hair and noses and mouths with clean cloths and took turns with the rug beater.

Have you ever seen the wire, fan-shaped rug beater with the wooden handle? You could sure build muscle with it!

The first one to swing (usually Dad) got lost in a cloud of dust. If every housewife in the neighborhood had decided to beat her rug the same day, I'm sure we would all have vanished in a cloud of dust.

We beat and beat until nothing emerged, and then the rug was laid on the grass and scrubbed, and you prayed no rain clouds would appear until it dried.

There was a bonus with this event.

The rug had been laid on newspapers; today, we have rug pads. Nothing was more fascinating than to read last year's newspapers, dusty as they were.

Without radio or TV, we read everything.

FOOD

Very few kids had to be coaxed to eat in that day. There was no instant food.

By the time dinner was on the table, we were ready because the tantalizing aroma had been saturating the house for at least an hour.

After school, even though you had a piece of home-made bread and jam, you were ready when the whole family sat down together and grace was said.

If Mom even anticipated you were going to leave anything on your plate, she said, "Eat everything—the people in Europe are starving."

Who these people were and why they were starving, we didn't know, but we sure felt we had somehow saved them by eating all our food.

CHICKEN

Chicken in my childhood meant only one thing—food. When someone said "chicken" to us, we didn't run home mad. We said, "Sure, I'll have a leg."

Do some of you know that there was a time you bought your chicken live?—not that sterile, pale body enclosed in plastic.

Have you ever seen a chicken hanging on a clothesline just after your father cut its head off with a sharp knife, and seen its body struggling to live and the blood oozing?

The next part of the act was mother dipping it in hot water and defeathering it and then relieving it of its entrails. Have you ever smelled wet feathers and the hot entrails of a chicken? "Ugh," is all I can say.

But when you got the delightful fragrance from the oven as it baked, you forgot the whole darn episode and enjoyed it. Why not? That was the only way you got chicken.

I could never understand why, when you undressed a chicken it was called "dressing a chicken."

The horrible, smelly, hot feathers when dried and fluffed became your pillows and your snuggly feather comforter that made sleeping in your bed like sleeping in your mother's womb.

We wasted nothing in our home.

AROMAS

Do you have in your memory the warm, sunny days in September when the windows and doors were all open (no air conditioning), and the air was filled with the lovely pungent smell of tomatoes being canned, catsup being made, grapes being readied for jelly?

In our neighborhood, the housewives prepared almost their whole stock of food and hoped it would last through the winter.

SAUERKRAUT

If you don't like it, don't read this. I couldn't stand your sarcasm.

In our cellar (we didn't call it a basement) stood a large brown ceramic crock waiting for cabbage-picking time. The cabbage was shredded, salted in layers, and when the crock was almost full, a rock was placed on the cabbage, and a board placed over the top of the crock. As it fermented, you ladled the ooze off, and when it was ready, we were ready.

Whenever Mom said, "What do you want for your birthday dinner?" I always said, "sauerkraut."

To this day, I would rather smell sauerkraut cooking than be offered a bottle of Chanel #5.

Bread baking—is there a more heavenly aroma? Bakers' bread was unknown to us.

Vinegar—the grocery store with the open pickle barrel —the salted fish that came in wooden buckets—the vinegar barrel.

KITCHEN

On the kitchen wall by the gas stove, with the oven on the same level as the burners, hung an ornate box with a hinged lid that held your salt.

Salt came in small, muslin bags.

Alongside this, was another container which held the box of kitchen matches.

A small hand pump provided water from the cistern or well. This was the only outlet of water in the house. The only source of hot water was the tea kettle on the stove.

We weren't under-privileged, as we had the most modern convenience available—gas.

We even had a gas iron that was connected to the gas jet by a hose, and you lit the interior of the iron with a match. This was the forerunner of the electric iron.

The kitchen table was covered with oil cloth. That's a word that has disappeared. Today we have plastic. The floor was covered with linoleum.

Saturday baths took place in a tub placed on the kitchen floor.

The kitchen served us in so many ways that one only had to place a bed in it, and you would have the efficiency apartment of today that costs a fortune.

THE PARLOR

The parlor was used only by guests and live and dead relatives.

The parlor was always closed off from the rest of the house. The furnishings usually were not made for comfort.

Instead of a coffee table, it had a library table.

Whenever a member of the family died, the coffin rested in the parlor, and a member of the family was always present to keep the dead company. Days after the funeral, the room held the odor of carnations.

However, on Sunday at our house, the parlor was open for the relatives who shared our Sunday dinner. After dinner, an aunt would play the upright chickering piano, and the Welsh voices would ring out.

The parlor held sad and happy memories.

THE OUTHOUSE

They still exist in some rustic places today, but they were a part of everyone's life in my small town until the sewer came through and the bathroom appeared.

We were proud of ours; we thought it a status symbol (of course then we didn't know the word). It was sturdily built, a three-holer. A budding artist in our community had painted on it a pastoral scene of cattails swaying in the breeze with lovely, white clouds floating in a blue sky. I guess you could have called it "interior decorating."

Imagine a cold wintry day, bundled up, walking the forty feet to this little, unheated, unlighted, but, oh, so necessary inconvenience!

There were no beautifully scented white or colored rolls of paper. No—there was the ever-present catalogue, not for reading purposes either—you hoped that the soft pages were still left, as the shiny pages were not very practical.

The daily newspaper also served. The big, Sunday edition took up the slack. My favorite section was the society page. I will leave this thought with my psychiatrist.

All your neighbors knew of your physical condition by the number of times you made the trip.

THE HONEYDIPPERS

Honeydippers—they came in the night.

Imagine walking home with your date on a warm summer night from a romantic movie (we walked everywhere), and you are filled with the thoughts of sweet love, and then a sickening sweet odor assails your nostrils and the heavy sound of horses' hooves and wagon wheels echoes in your ears, and your heart sinks.

You both pretend you do not hear or smell anything. But there they were, slowly passing you on their way to the nightly cleaning of the ever-present outhouses.

The most necessary and most avoided men in your life—the honeydippers.

SWIMMING POOLS

There weren't any.

Within walking distance (any place two or three miles was walking distance, as walking was our main source of transportation), there was always a stream that was dammed-up in the summer to create a pool.

This was the boys' delight, and they, of course, had no bathing suits. They weren't on the market in our neighborhood, and the boys skinny-dipped.

One day, an adventurous friend (who had acquired that new invention—the automobile) invited the family for a ride, and, as we passed a swimming hole, my brother emerged, naked, and chased after us down the road.

He wasn't going to miss this great adventure.

At a time when bodies were not spoken of, this was a great embarrassment to all of us—even if he was only nine.

GAMES

"Run, Sheep, Run" was the name of the game.

Today the neighbors would have called the cops. This usually took place after supper (no one on our social level ate dinner except at noon). We ran like sheep through the neighbors' yards.

"Lemonade" was played in the street.

Everyone could hear a horse coming. Cars were almost non-existent. "Lemonade" was a form of charades.

Tin cans with holes punched in them and a string through, long enough to reach your hands, were used for stilt walking.

Spinning tops was a part of your life.

The more adventurous would ask a smiling adult to "Throw a penny." If the penny was forthcoming, the first to plug it got the coin.

Even in those days, kids threw money away. The thrill was to put a penny on the streetcar track for the streetcar to flatten it.

Hide and Seek, Hopscotch, Jacks (for the girls), and, of course, marbles were a part of every boy's life.

HALLOWEEN

Halloween lasted a whole week.

Monday night was corn night. Dried ears of corn were shucked and the grains thrown at the windows to frighten the people inside.

Tuesday was cabbage night. The cabbage, still left in the gardens, was garnered, and the leaves thrown on the porches.

Wednesday night, you took the tic-tac-toes you made by chipping empty thread spools and winding a string around them, and you pulled them down the windows. You hoped the noise inside would be frightening, except it was expected.

Thursday, you did the dirty work—the soaping. No dirty words, just marks.

If Friday was Halloween, you dressed up in homemade costumes (even the adults), and went "trick and treating."

However, on Halloween night, the big boys had their kicks by pushing over an outhouse here and there, and heaven help the needy person who went to make a "call of nature."

JULY 4TH

July 4th meant fireworks, a neighborhood parade to the local playground, free tickets for lemonade and wiener sandwiches, and the carousel brought in for the great day.

It was ushered in at daybreak by the loud boom of a homemade cannon set off in an open field by some of the young men. This was the moment you had been waiting for.

For weeks, you hoarded your pennies and nickels you had earned running errands, to buy spitdevils, sparklers, little red cylinders strung on a string that went off in a series, little cones that, when lit, grew in the form of a snake.

You always bought a piece of punk that, once lit, made the lighting of your treasure easier. You earned this treasure, so you took care to make it last the day.

Every house on our street was a picture in red, white and blue bunting-wrapped pillars, potatoes hanging pierced with small flags, and the big flag hanging from the center of the porch.

In the evening, the fathers put off the rockets and the pinwheels, and we twirled the sparklers.

Once we had an extra thrill. One rocket took off too low and entered the window of a neighbor's house and landed in a sack of quilt patches. Little damage was done, but in our quiet lives it was a topic of conversation for weeks.

In our state now, fireworks for individuals are banned. I miss the noise.

SERENADE

A delightful custom in our neighborhood was the serenade.

When a couple returned to the bride's home after the honeymoon, every kid in the neighborhood was alerted, and some of the adults, and they arrived from blocks around with tin cans, which they beat with sticks. You had better be prepared with sacks of candy for each one, as this noise went on until every can-carrying individual got his treat.

I swear these kids had radar in their heads, as the arrival almost coincided with the arrival of the honeymooners.

OUTDOOR MOVIES

We had them in our neighborhood (silent ones, of course).

Several of the fathers, including mine, were responsible for a playground in our neighborhood.

Playgrounds were rare.

In the summer on Thursday nights, a screen was erected and a silent movie shown.

We stood the whole time, as there were no chairs. But we were a hardy bunch of kids, and so enthralled by this marvelous invention that I think we would have stood on our heads if we had to.

A very important fact to our parents was that this was free. I wish I knew who paid for them, but of course, then, I didn't care.

We had many community-spirited fathers in our community.

MOVIES

Saturday was the biggest day of the week.

Twenty-five cents was our allowance for doing our chores. This meant two movies and a wiener sandwich. I just missed the nickelodeon era; the movies had inflated to ten cents.

We went first to the Court to see *Pearl White,* a continued thriller, and we left her every Saturday either tied on a railroad track or in a room with water coming up to her chin.

We screamed and stomped until we were emotionally exhausted, and the lady playing the piano drove us into hysteria with the appropriate music. (Silent movies were just that—silent.)

The music was provided by local talent.

Then, calmed down by the wiener sandwich, we went to the Bijou to see *The Thirteen Brides* or some other thriller, and again we screamed and pounded our feet.

No wonder we went quietly to bed on Saturday night, and behaved somewhat decorously in Sunday School the next day.

We were emotionally exhausted.

PROGRESS

With the advent of the sewer and electric power my world changed rapidly.

Every family in the neighborhood either had a room built onto their home to be called "the bathroom" or utilized an extra bedroom.

A great boon to Mom was the electric washer.

The horse began to disappear and the automobile took over.

Radio opened a new world and people stayed home from the shows to hear "Amos and Andy."

We could no longer live in the innocence of our own immediate neighborhood. The tragedies of the whole world were being thrust upon us.

The changes in our lives were so quick and so radical, that my sister, nine years younger than I, could not have experienced the things I have written.